The Ralph STEADman
BOOK OF
DOGS

The Ralph STEADman

Book of

DOGS

ATLANTIC BOOKS

LONDON

DOMESTIC
FOX HUNTING
Ralph STEADman 2005
to the LOOSE MANOR
BORN.

First published in Great Britain in 2010 by Atlantic Books,
an imprint of Atlantic Books Ltd.

9 8 7 6 5 4 3 2 1

A CIP catalogue record for this book is available
from the British Library.

ISBN: 978 1 84887 675 0

Book design by Simon McFadden
Cover design by Henry Steadman

Printed in Great Britain

Atlantic Books
An imprint of Grove Atlantic Ltd
Ormond House
26–27 Boswell Street
London
WC1N 3JZ

www.atlantic-books.co.uk

DOUBLE DOG

Introduction

To do another book about dogs in the wake of my three
other books about dogs is, I am aware, a trifle excessive.
Well, it would seem so but then I heard a report that there
are, at least, fifty million more dogs in the United Kingdom
alone and their owners are going to need more vital wisdom
about these faithful but stupid creatures that will help them
to sustain a sense of humour – not to mention proportion –
if they are going to treat their mutts right and give them a
half-decent life and, most importantly, see the funny side of
their every action.

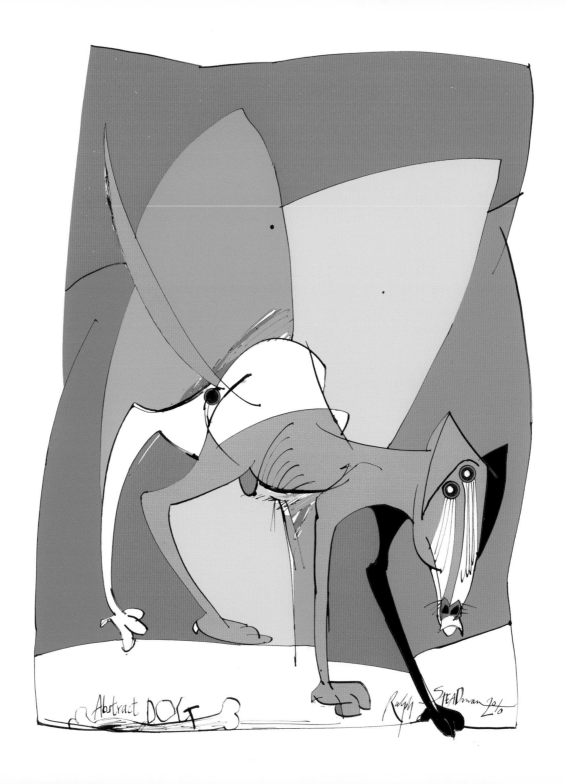

Abstract DOG

Ralph STEADman 2010

The point is, I WAS going to do a book about Ferrets, since they are, I believe, the third most common uncaged pet on the planet, but this was discouraged on the grounds that the average book-buying reader doesn't like Ferrets and, indeed, they harbour an aversion to the poor little critters. The reason, I believe has something to do with their habits of tunnelling – which means diving through recesses between books, making nests amongst books and chewing the classics, particularly around the edges – and with first editions taking priority. So, I thought, forget Ferrets. What about white mice? No! Same sort of problem. Rabbits are cuddly but boring. Rats? UGH!!

NO THANK YOU!! Orangutans climb all over the place.
Pygmy Goats need a proper farmyard and Turtles
are too slow. Then I thought of the Hahn's Macaw
but nobody knew what they looked like – I mentioned
the big beaks and that put people off too!
Chipmunks, Llamas (mmmm?), Degus (what the
hell are they?), Chinchillas, exotic or Chameleons
(I wouldn't know what to say about them
except that they change colour – so not a good
choice for artistic consistency).

DOUBLE DOG

Adult Bearded Dragons sound like a good idea and so do Pythons but why make problems for yourself? Pigeons are everywhere and are just a bloody mess – so you see – I am back to Dogs – man's best friend! Anyway, I have already started and have a whole new series of doggy impressions which will delight and intrigue a whole new generation of Dog-book collectors. A lot of folks wont have seen the first three books so they may go look for them in second-hand bookshops … etc!

February 2010

SPOT with friends.   Ralph STEADman 20/

BLOG 4 — MAN'S BEST FRIEND BUT ONE!

BLOT DOT -5 — MAKING FRIENDS   Ralph STEADman 2010

BLOT DOG 6 - ALLOW IT'S ANGER TO SUBSIDE - BEFORE STROKING

Ralph STEADman 2/5

BLOT DOG 7 — ANTI-SOCIAL BLOG

BLOT DOG 8.— A TYPE
OF CROSSBREED

CROSS° BREED — VERY ANNOYED

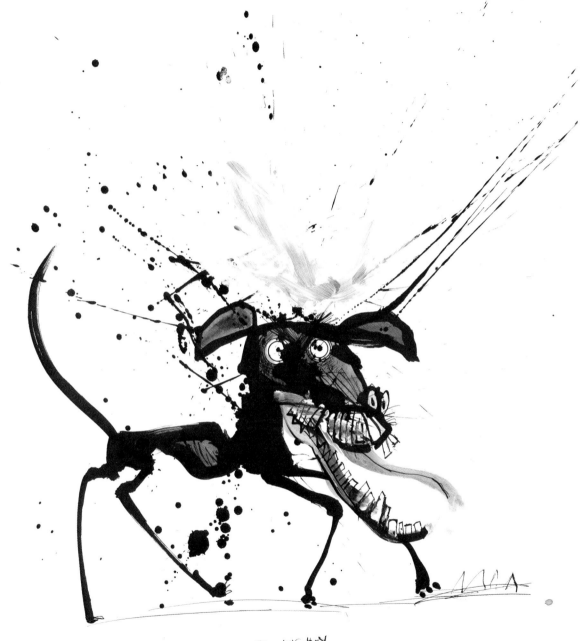

CROSS BREED—2 NAUGHTY, NAUGHTY

OVERBREEDING
—THE WORST EFFECTS —EXPLOSIVE FLATULENCE

Ralph STEADman 2012

INSTANT
RECOGNITION

Ralph STEADman 2%

GOOD
DOGS-1

FUNDAMENTALIST DOG

A PRIZE-WINNING BITCH.

.... IN OUR MODERN WORLD OF LOWERED STANDARDS
AND THE CULT OF THE 3RD RATE, IT IS THE FIRM
RESOLVE OF A DEDICATED PAWFUL...

IN ALL PURSUITS,
IN ALL AREAS OF HUMAN
ENDEAVOUR, THERE ARE
THOSE WHO WILL SETTLE
FOR NOTHING LESS THAN
PERFECTION....

Reduce Intelligence

Acme/Sybil & Audrey FRIDAY.

Mark 1 GROOMER.

SHAITAS and II (Gouge in next litter.

Mark II GROOMER / GAVEL

DRAIN HERE.

THE CUSTODIANS OF THESE MODISHLY
STYLED CREATURES ARE OUR BULWARKS AGAINST
NATURE'S FUMBLING COMMONPLACE.

BREEDS TO AVOID.

'NOISELESS FLATULENCE' CAN BE A REAL SOCIAL EMBARRASSMENT AND IS COMMON IN BIG DOGS WHOSE DIETS ARE SUPPLEMENTED IN BULK WITH GRAIN + SOY BEAN PRODUCTS. ONE IS NEVER SURE OF THE CULPRIT AND THE POOR OWNER IS BLAMED MORE OFTEN THAN NOT QUITE UNFAIRLY. UNFORTUNATELY THE ONLY CURE FOR THIS CONDITION IS A LONGER LEAD AND FAITHFUL DOGS TEND TO HANG ABOUT CLOSE TO THEIR OWNERS ON SUCH OCCASIONS.

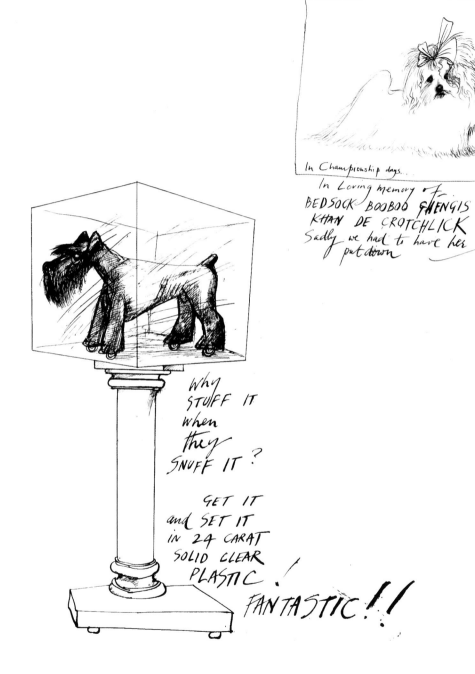

In Championship days.

In Loving memory of
BEDSOCK BOOBOO GHENGIS
KHAN DE CROTCHLICK
Sadly we had to have her
put down

A week ago...

— we'll never
forget you,
BEDSOCK.

Why
STUFF IT
when
they
SNUFF IT?

GET IT
and SET IT
IN 24 CARAT
SOLID CLEAR
PLASTIC!

FANTASTIC!!

HOW TO TREAT YOUR DOG AND DISCIPLINE ~~IIII~~ IT: **2**
TEACHING YOUR DOG TO TAKE A BATH MAY NEED MORE
RESTRAINT THAN YOU HAVE HANDS FOR. BATH CLAMPS
ARE A MUST, OTHERWISE YOU'LL GET THE BATH AND
THE DOG WILL PUT THE REST OF THE WATER ON YOUR
WALL.

SIGNS TO WATCH FOR:

If a dog goes off its food or vomits, coughs, discharges from the eyes, seems lethargic or simply lies down and stops breathing, immediate action is necessary. Don't wait for the VET. He is invariably overworked, sick like your dog, or involved in a road accident on his way over.

ARTIFICIAL RESPIRATION SHOULD BE ATTEMPTED IF A SWIFT KICK IN THE RIBS DOESN'T DO THE TRICK

The old-fashioned method of rhythmic pressure to the rib cage can work, but in the case of small dogs, mouth to mouth respiration is very popular with modern dog-owners.

This is NOT advisable with big dogs. Wait for the VET. He gets PAID for it!

TAKING A DOG'S TEMPERATURE:

NOBODY WOULD BE FOOLISH ENOUGH TO PRETEND THAT SUCH A PROCEDURE IS A DODDLE. A DOG'S TEMPERATURE IS TAKEN RECTALLY. TRY TO IMAGINE YOURSELF CORNERED BY SOMEONE WHOM YOU THOUGHT WAS A FRIEND, HOLDING A LONG GLASS TUBE FULL OF MERCURY AND SMEARED WITH VASELINE, TELLING YOU IN CHINESE THAT THEY ARE GOING TO STICK IT UP YOUR BACKSIDE— FOR NO APPARENT REASON....

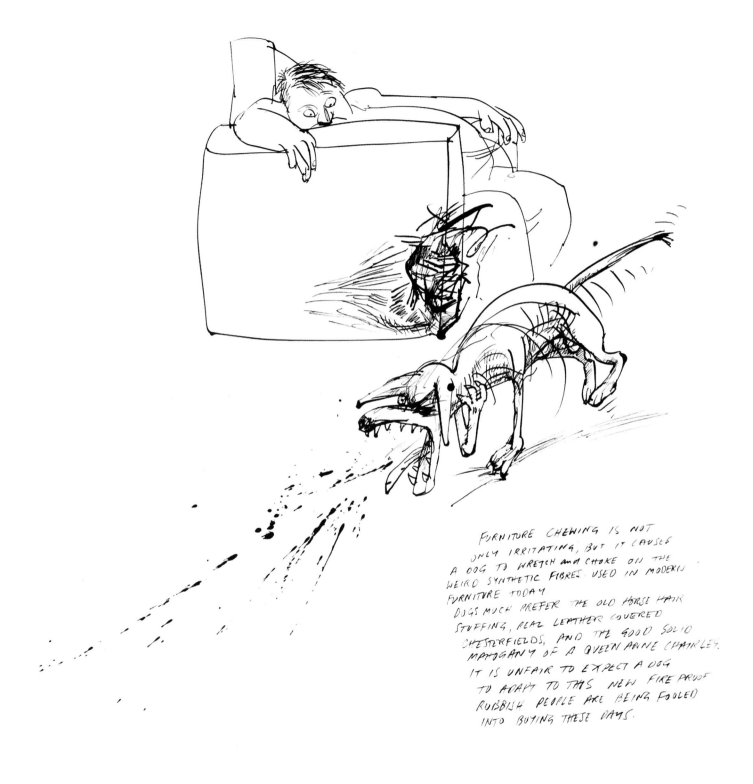

FURNITURE CHEWING IS NOT
ONLY IRRITATING, BUT IT CAUSES
A DOG TO WRETCH and CHOKE ON THE
WEIRD SYNTHETIC FIBRES USED IN MODERN
FURNITURE TODAY
DOGS MUCH PREFER THE OLD HORSE HAIR
STUFFING, REAL LEATHER COVERED
CHESTERFIELDS, AND THE GOOD SOLID
MAHOGANY OF A QUEEN ANNE CHAIRLEG.
IT IS UNFAIR TO EXPECT A DOG
TO ADAPT TO THIS NEW FIRE PROOF
RUBBISH PEOPLE ARE BEING FOOLED
INTO BUYING THESE DAYS.

SIGNS TO WATCH FOR:
When your dog is hungry the reason
is often not simply lack of FOOD — but
VARIETY.
  If he chews ~~his~~ his leg off and brings it
to you he may be trying to tell you
that he has had enough of the same old
thing. If after remedial action the
condition still persists and
he chews another leg off, then
he probably wants WHEELS.

VOLCANIC WINE DOG No 12 Pantelleria

SIGNS TO WATCH FOR: 5
'THAT LOOK' IS A DOG'S STRONGEST
WEAPON, AND THE DOG KNOWS IT.
THE SWINE WILL MELT YOU
MERCILESSLY WITH JUNGLE CUNNING
TO GET WHAT IT WANTS. HOWEVER
YOU DEAL WITH IT THE LOOK
PREVAILS. ONLY IN A DRAWING CAN
YOU OBLITERATE IT — AND EVEN
THEN IT WHIMPERS THROUGH.
SO BEWARE OF IT — AND THE
FIRST SIGN — SHOVE THE BUGGER
IN THE WOOD SHED!

BEANIE

Jackson - Joe PETRO's POOch.

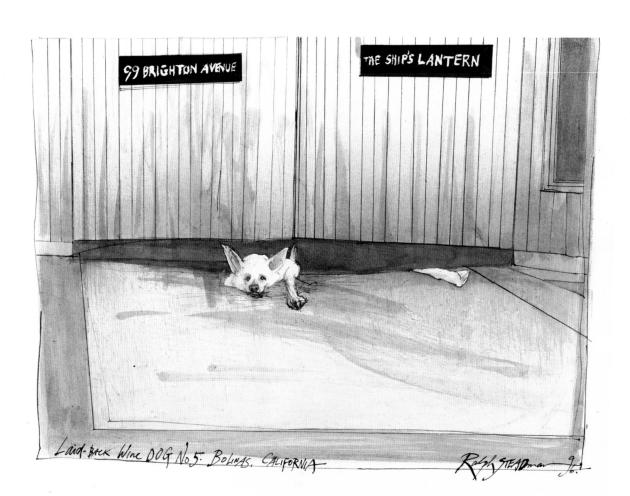

Laid-Back Wine DOG No5. BOLINAS, CALIFORNIA   Ralph STEADman 96.

FLOP AT WORK   Ralph Steadman

STAY FLOP!

FLOP SMILING

FLOP
TRIES TO
SMILE.

FLOP UNCERTAIN
ABOUT WHAT I
WANT DO NEXT.

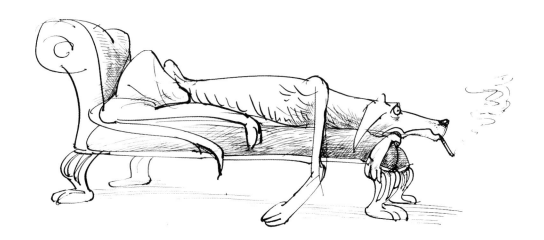

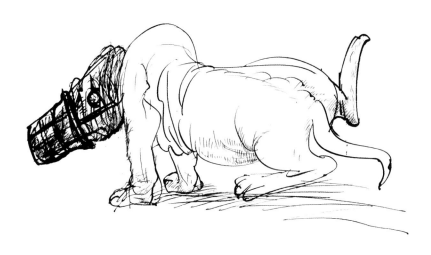

WANTED—FOR GOOD FAITHFUL DOG—NEW WORTHLESS OWNERS.

Ralph STEADman 2010

Man leading
his blind dog specially
bought for him by ~~the~~ ~~the the~~ kindly donations.

WOOF!

DOG·BABY SUBSTITUTE

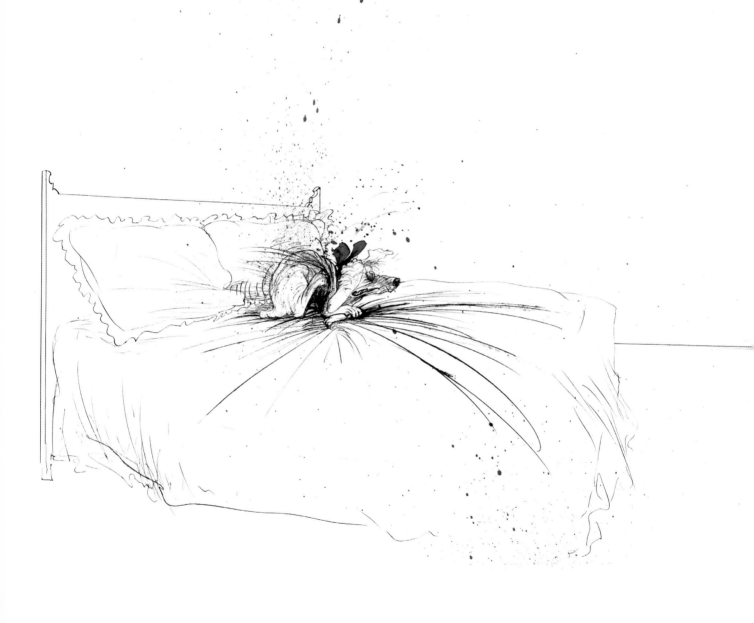

Old Scratch

DOGFIGHT—DIDDLELY SQUAT!

A RABID DOG
AND FRIEND

BHUDDIST DOGS LOOKING FOR HAPPINESS

The HINDU DOG   This is BRAHMAN!
                                 Ralph STEADman 2015

MANDARIN DOG   Ralph STEADman 2000

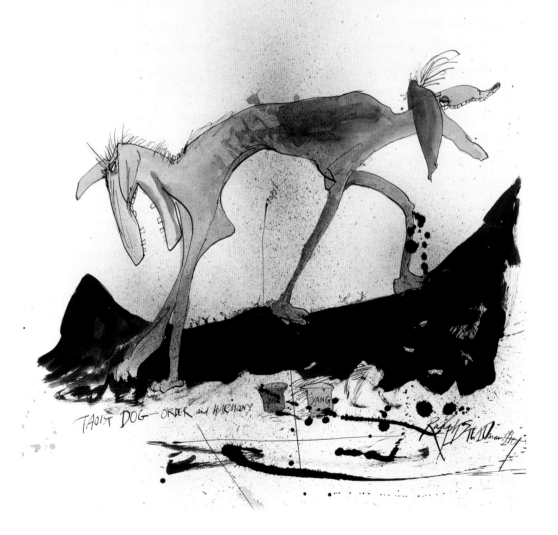

TAOIST DOG — ORDER and HARMONY

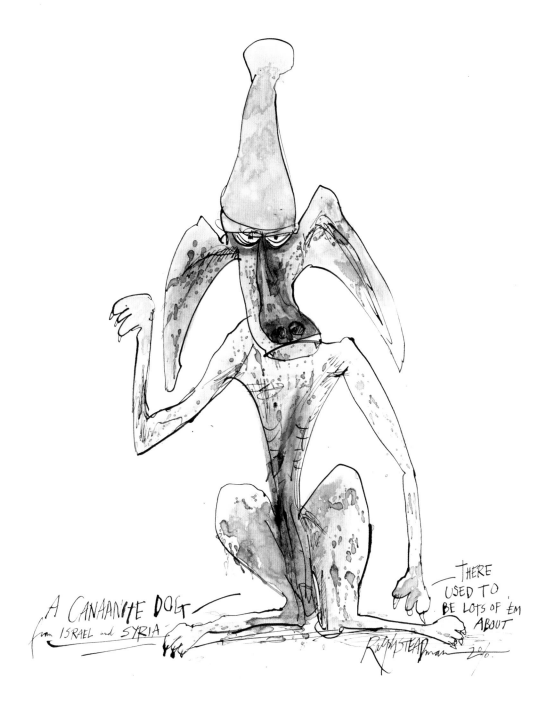

A CANAANITE DOG
from ISRAEL and SYRIA

THERE
USED TO
BE LOTS OF 'EM
ABOUT

RalphSTEADman 2010.

Zaroustrian DOG Zarothustering with Sacred FLAME to banish the DARK

DOG COLLAR

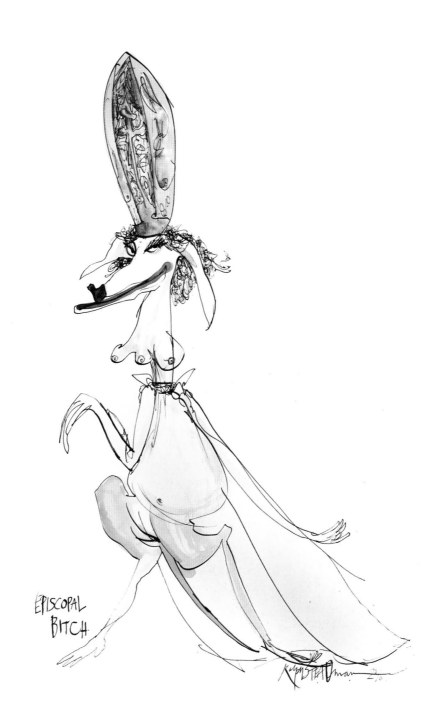

EPISCOPAL
BITCH

DOG DAYS. ----- Ralph Steadman 2008

MATALONG BUTEROS.
Bolivia 2010

CUTEE
POO

2010

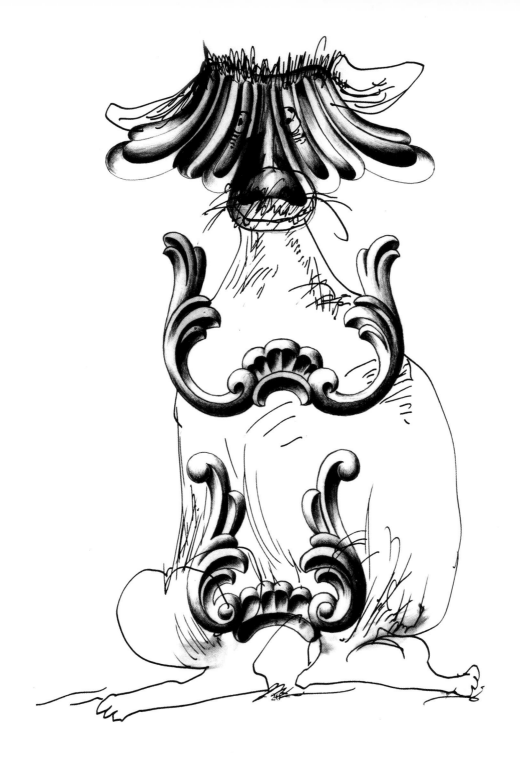

DECIBELLE
THE NOISY
MONGREL

LOVE ME—
LOVE MY MASTER

DOG ATTACKS MAN IN RED PANTS. Ralph STEADman 2010